DATE DUE			

C.1

2633

by D. L. Mabery

George Lucas

Lerner Publications Company
Minneapolis

Photo credits:

Tri-Star Pictures, pp. 1, 10, 37; Fotos International, pp. 4, 20; Movie Star News, pp. 8, 32; MJJ Productions, p. 13; Museum of Modern Art/Film Stills Archives, p. 16; Collectors Book Store, pp. 17, 24; Ralph Nelson Jr./Fotos International, p. 28; Richard Young/Retna Ltd., p. 30; AP/Wide World Photos, p. 31; Walt Disney Corp., pp. 34, 38
Front cover photographs by Fotos International and (inset) Tri-Star Pictures, Inc.; back cover photograph by Ralph Nelson Jr./Fotos International

Manufactured in the United States of America

LIBRARY OF CONGRESS CATALOGING-IN-PUBLICATION DATA

Mabery, D.L.
  George Lucas.

  Summary: Traces the life of the film maker who directed such movies as "American Graffiti" and "Star Wars."
  1. Lucas, George—Juvenile literature. 2. Moving-picture producers and directors—United States—Biography—Juvenile literature. [1. Lucas, George. 2. Motion picture producers and directors]   I. Title.
  PN1998.A3L855   1987   791.43'0233'0924 [92] [B]   86-33708
  ISBN 0-8225-1614-4

1 2 3 4 5 6 7 8 9 10 97 96 95 94 93 92 91 90 89 88 87

Contents

HIGH SPEED

There once was a time when George Lucas didn't think about making movies. In fact, his childhood dreams were focused more clearly upon car racing. George was born May 14, 1944, and grew up in Modesto, California, a town fifty miles east of San Francisco. Like a lot of California towns in that region, Modesto is characterized by wide streets and almost endless suburbs. To pass the time, kids cruised up and down Main Street and listened to their car radios. And George grew up no different from any of the other kids.

George's father, who owned a stationery store in Modesto, believed in the virtues of "early to bed and early to rise." George, Sr., tried to instill these virtues in his three daughters and one son. But it seemed like George, Jr., never listened. He spent a lot of time alone, reading comic books or watching Saturday morning cartoons. George's father said, "He was hard to understand. He was always dreaming up things."

George was also one of those students who didn't do very well in school, though his attendance record during high school was remarkable. One school counselor remembers that George was at school every day. The boy didn't contribute much to class, but he was always there watching.

Still, some of George's teachers recognized that there was something in his mind that would probably develop later in life. Lucas's mother recalls being pulled aside by George's art teacher at one parent-teacher conference. "You have no idea the ability this boy has," the teacher said.

Yet George didn't really show much interest in anything except cars. He was on the tennis team, but his mother thought it was a shame George would have so few school activities to list in his yearbook. She encouraged him to try out for the senior class play. Lucas got a small part and began attending rehearsals. Then the set designer became sick, and George became involved creating sets and props. Part of the talent his art teacher had noticed was brought to the surface.

The play's director was impressed with George's work, and encouraged him to continue, yet Lucas still had the notion of becoming a race car driver. That dream was shattered on June 12, 1962, three days before his high school graduation. Driving back home from the library, George took a route through some pastureland and a walnut grove. He was racing his Fiat, driving over sixty miles per hour down the country roads.

George started to make the left-hand turn onto the dirt road to his parents' house. One of the Lucases' neighbors, a seventeen-year-old kid, was coming down the road in the opposite direction. His Chevy Impala slammed into George's car broadside. The impact tossed the Fiat sideways and flipped the car four times before it came to rest wrapped around a walnut tree. The racing seatbelt George had installed in his car gave way, and he was hurled out of the open roof of the car on the third flip.

The accident crushed both his lungs, and he lay in the hospital for three days before the doctors were sure he would survive. He missed graduation, and took four months to struggle back to good health.

During the long summer of recuperation, many ideas and thoughts went through George's mind. He discovered his personal power to survive. As he began to get well, he realized that each person has his or her own energy to create momentum and realize goals. Within this energy, George decided, there is both good and bad. A person has the choice between the two, but the world would certainly work better if people would choose the good. What George had discovered was what he called "the Force."

George discusses the Force with Alec Guinness (left), who played Obi-Wan Kenobi, on the set of *Star Wars.*

Years later, George Lucas would have the characters of *Star Wars* explain the Force in easier terms. Ben Obi-Wan Kenobi, one of the last of the gentle and perfect Jedi knights, explained the Force to young Luke Skywalker this way: "It is an energy field and something more. An aura that at once controls and obeys. It is a nothingness that can accomplish miracles."

Having accomplished the miracle of recuperation after nearly being killed in his automobile accident, Lucas entered Modesto Junior College and studied sociology and anthropology.

George also started playing around with a small movie camera. Instead of racing cars, he filmed them. He made trick animation, and ran his films backwards. Two years later, with encouragement by a photographer who had worked on a number of Hollywood movies, George enrolled in the film school of the University of Southern California in Los Angeles.

It was at the USC film school that young George Lucas realized what it was he wanted to do with his life. He wanted to make movies.

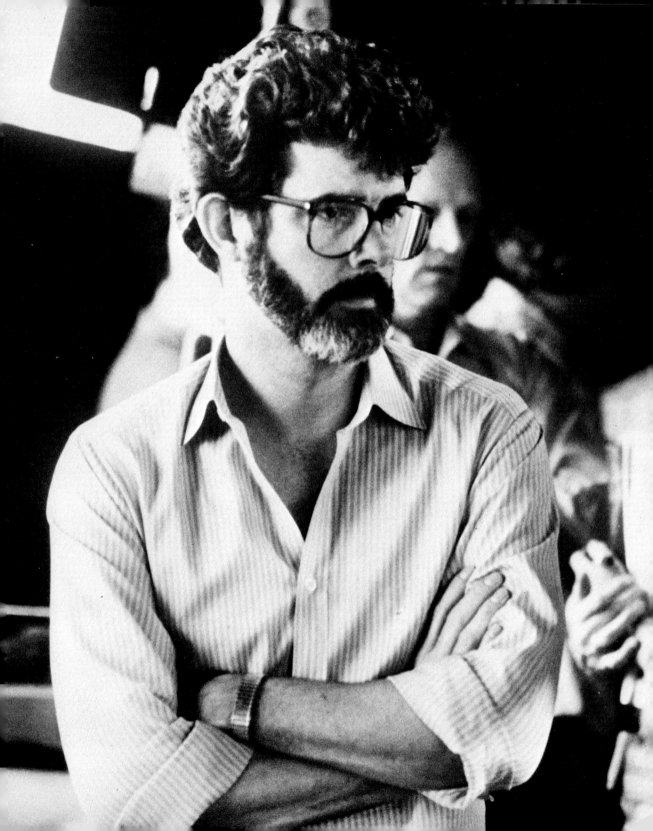

DEVELOPING A CINEMATIC EYE

The films George Lucas made while in film school were free-form, experimental films with no story or plot. One of the films, a graduate student project, was a science fiction movie titled *THX 1138:4EB (Electronic Labyrinth)*. Set in the future, his movie was a depressing look at society. George's story had people living underground, and everyone's name replaced by a number.

George's *THX 1138:4EB* won first prize at the National Student Film Festival in 1967, which earned the young director a six-month scholarship to observe filmmaking at Warner Bros. studio. Having grown up watching Warner Bros.' Looney Tune cartoons of Bugs Bunny and Roadrunner, George was eager to spend his time in the animation department.

The day George arrived at Warner Bros. was the day

11

Jack Warner, head of the studio, was leaving because the studio had been sold to a corporation. "The whole place was shutting down," George remembers. "They were only making one movie, *Finian's Rainbow*, so that's where I ended up."

Finian's Rainbow was being directed by Francis Ford Coppola, a young director who had been five years ahead of Lucas in the film school across town. While at UCLA, Coppola had somehow managed to get his student film, *You're a Big Boy Now*, distributed as a major feature film. And now the young man was directing a major motion picture for one of Hollywood's greatest studios. George was in awe.

"You see, we were taught that nobody ever got a job in the industry," Lucas said. George thought students graduated from film school, and became ticket takers at Disneyland while waiting for the chance to direct television commercials. Francis Coppola was directing a *picture* fresh out of school. "It sent shock waves through the student film world, because nobody else had ever done that."

George became Francis's assistant, observing how a major Hollywood picture was directed. A film's director determines the camera angles for each scene being photographed and tells the actors where to move and when. The director usually works closely with the film's producer, who is the person responsible for bringing the film crews together and is in charge of the money for the production. Because the producer keeps tabs on the money, she or he will decide how much can be spent on costumes, sets, stunts, and actors' salaries.

After a film has been shot, it goes into what is called "post-production." During this stage, the film is edited. That means the scenes the director wants to use are cut out from the reels of film and put together with other scenes in the right sequence. Editing is very crucial. The editor must know what is important in the scene, when to cut the film and in which order the edited bits

Michael Jackson, Francis Coppola, and George Lucas mugging for the camera after they completed *Captain EO* **together in 1986.**

13

of film should go together. Bad editing can make even a well-written and acted film seem slow and boring, or so fast and jerky that it makes no sense.

At Warner Bros., George and Francis hit it off well. After all, they had a lot in common—both were in their twenties, both were bearded, and both had a dream of setting up their own studio some day. Together, Lucas has said, they were like two halves of a whole. But George soon became restless and was eager to start on a project of his own.

Coppola told Lucas that if he wanted to direct films, he first had to learn how to write a script. George wanted to expand his student film *THX* with the help of a major studio, so he set about writing a new "treatment." A film treatment is an outline of the proposed action of a script. Meanwhile, Coppola offered George a job on *Finian's Rainbow* and on the next film he was planning, *The Rain People*. In return, Coppola said he would help Lucas with *THX*. George agreed.

Francis was the writer and director for *The Rain People*, a story about a housewife escaping suburban life by driving across the country. Lucas served as assistant cameraman, art director, and film editor. They began shooting with a small crew and a small budget. Francis made sure that George kept working on his script for *THX* as well.

When *Rain People* was finished, Francis borrowed money from Warner Bros. to set up his own filmmaking facility in an old warehouse in San Francisco. His idea was to create the same type of creative atmosphere as he had found in film school. He wanted a place where filmmakers could work, cooperate, and exchange ideas. Francis was president and George was vice president. Francis called the company American Zoetrope.

The first Zoetrope project was George's *THX*. When George turned in his script, he said, "This is terrible." Francis read it and said, "You're right." So the pair hired an outside writer to finish the screenplay. Even with screenwriting help, it looked like Francis and George could not sell the science fiction idea to any Hollywood studio. So George began to work on a different idea with a screenwriter he knew from film school. He called the story, about the war in Vietnam, *Apocalypse Now.*

Meanwhile, Francis approached Warner Bros. again with *THX.* He took the script, some graphics designed by Lucas, and footage from George's student film of the story. He also threw into the deal Lucas's idea for the Vietnam movie. This time Warner said yes.

In November 1969, George began shooting a new version of his student film. He was to be paid $15,000 to write and direct it. In this version, after the earth's surface became uninhabitable, humans had to go underground. There they lived in a technological beehive. George filmed the movie in San Francisco's newly-built subway system before it was put into operation.

"I realized that we were already living in the future

that everyone was talking and writing about in the 1930s," George told *Newsweek* magazine at the time. "I thought, 'Hey, I can do a science fiction movie using real locations.'"

George edited together a rough cut of *THX*, which is a version of a movie without a musical sound track and with the scenes edited together just to see how the story works. Francis took the rough cut, the finished script for *Apocalypse Now*, and six other projects to Warner Bros. in Los Angeles. Warner Bros. took one

THX 1138 **was a bleak, cold movie. Here Robert Duvall confronts security guards.**

A scene from the sock hop dance in *American Graffiti,* **with Ron Howard and Cindy Williams**

look at *THX* and the other projects and said it was all junk. And that they wanted their money back. Coppola and Lucas call the day "Black Thursday."

THX 1138 was finally released on March 11, 1971, although not in the version George originally intended. Movie critics thought George's movie was sophisticated and technically brilliant. However, it didn't do very well at the box office.

One of the reasons *THX* failed at the box office, Lucas decided, was because its view of life in the future was too grim. "Everyone thought I was cold and wierd,"

George remembers. "Why didn't I do something warm and human?" So for his next project, he decided to make a movie about the lives of the high school class of 1962. He called it *American Graffiti*.

Because of the reputation of *THX*, George's *American Graffiti* was turned down by every studio in Hollywood. Finally, Universal Studios agreed to put the movie out if George would use a big Hollywood "name" to produce it.

In the meantime, Francis had directed *The Godfather*, a story about the Mafia, for Paramount Studios. Coppola had only accepted the job because of his debts. Ironically, *The Godfather* had become the biggest hit of 1972 and is considered by many critics to be one of the best American movies ever made. Francis was now considered "hot," and he was the "name" Universal suggested to produce *Graffiti*. George agreed.

American Graffiti was shot in twenty-eight days during June and July 1972. For his work, George was paid even less than he had received for *THX*. The story takes place all in one night, and centers around a group of high school friends before they leave for college. The movie contains two key elements Lucas remembered from his own teenage years: cruising around in cars, and listening to rock 'n' roll music.

Lucas showed his film to Universal Studios executives and a special preview audience on January 28, 1973. As the credits rolled at the end of the movie, the audience's applause was rapturous. Universal's executives, however,

18

hated the film. The top executive said, "This is in no shape to show to an audience!"

George was in shock. He remembered the troubles he had gone through with *THX*, and he felt like he was about to lose control of another film. Francis started screaming at the executive: "You should get down on your knees and thank George. He did this film for nothing, and he killed himself getting it done! Couldn't you say, 'Thank you, you did sort of a good job. Glad you brought it in on budget and on time'?"

George fought with the studio for eight months to release the film. During this time, George's wife, Marcia, a film editor, was supporting the couple. George had met Marcia in 1967 when they had both worked on editing films for a government agency, and they had been married in 1969. In the end, Universal only cut four and a half minutes from *American Graffiti*, and it was released in August 1973.

No one was prepared for the reaction *American Graffiti* caused at the box office. George's grand celebration of adolescent life struck a responsive chord in audiences, and the movie became the biggest hit of the year. For every dollar spent making the movie, Universal saw more than fifty dollars return in profits.

Now some of Hollywood's movie studios were willing to listen to the young director. He set about working on his "little space movie," a movie that would alter the history of films.

IN A FAR, FAR GALAXY

"Space is the final frontier, as someone famous once said. For anybody who has looked up at the stars, it has been a fascination since mankind could think," Lucas says. "When I was young, I looked up and said 'What's up there?'"

George's curiosity for what lay out beyond the reaches of our current space exploration fostered an idea that brought about his greatest success.

Even before George made *American Graffiti*, he had an idea for a space adventure movie. The movie was *Star Wars*, and when it was released on May 25, 1977, it became the biggest money-making film in the history of Hollywood up to that time. (That record was broken in 1982 by George's friend Steven Spielberg's film *E.T.*) The style of *Star Wars* also influenced the way in which movies would be made.

21

Star Wars' story is pretty simple. It is a fairy tale about a country boy who dreams of adventure, and finds himself smack in the middle of a battle of good against evil. But George used themes from ancient myths in his script, which helped broaden the film's appeal. Myths have been described as a way of communicating the most basic unconscious concerns, such as taking risks and learning to tell right from wrong. And George took the myth of testing and triumph and placed it in outer space. He succeeded in touching deep beliefs common to all humanity.

The other significant fact about *Star Wars* is the visual language the film created with the state-of-the-arts special effects. Special effects in movies really depend as much on the widest range of science and technology as they do on filmmaking. Also, with this movie George got to put his talent as an animator to use.

Each of *Star Wars'* special effects required the use of more than one camera. In some cases, as many as twelve cameras were used. The spacecrafts, for example, would be shot by one camera. The animated laser beams would be shot at a different time. These individual shots would be added to one another, one layer at a time, until the final scene had been created.

Sandwiching film together was nothing new at the time George was directing *Star Wars*. What was innovative, however, was the use of computers to control the shots. The *Millenium Falcon* which Han Solo pilots never moved on the set. Its swoops through deep space were created by a camera that rotated around a small model of the spaceship. The camera's rotations were controlled by a computer, so that each shot could be duplicated exactly or changed slightly and precisely.

"To get special effects right," Lucas has said, "you really should shoot them two or three times before you figure out exactly how it should work."

The visual style of *Star Wars* is also one of quick cuts from one scene to another. The movie does not stop for a lot of explanation. This style is unlike that of most movies. George felt that modern movie audiences, who were used to watching fast-paced television shows and television commercials, which get an idea across with pictures and music, were able to perceive visual information presented quickly.

The breakneck pace of George's movies came about, he says, because of his fascination with car racing and high speed.

The sound in *Star Wars* was also unlike anything else that was being done at the time. The voice for Chewbacca, for instance, was created by combining the sounds of a bear's growl, a walrus's grunt, a seal's bark, a tiger's roar, and a lizard's hiss.

For Darth Vader's voice, Lucas wanted a sound that was "like a walking iron lung." Darth Vader is supposed to have been badly burned and to be forced to keep his body encased in his suit in order to stay alive. To get

On location in the Tunisian desert to shoot *Star Wars,* **George (second from left) and his crew wore goggles to shield their eyes from blowing sand. Even the camera was wrapped in plastic.**

the right mechanical sound for the voice, sound technicians placed a tiny microphone inside the breathing regulator of scuba diving gear.

In addition, there are 90 minutes of music in *Star Wars,* which runs 110 minutes. Lucas said his idea for having music throughout the film came from the famous symphony *Peter and the Wolf*. In that symphony, characters such as Peter, the Wolf, a Duck, and so forth, are represented by different instruments in the orchestra. *Star Wars* used the same idea of identifying each character with a specific sound. "We did it so that each character has their own theme and whenever that character is on the screen, that theme is played."

As spectacular as *Star Wars* is, George says it is only twenty-five percent of the movie he wanted to make. He couldn't afford to make the kind of movie he wanted, so he had to settle for less.

When you look at the space battle in the first movie, George has pointed out, the ships move very slowly, and there aren't more than two or three ships in a shot. He achieved the effect that there was a complicated battle going on by his editing, with a lot of quick cuts and cross-cutting. He had the same sort of limits with the creatures in the cantina Han Solo and Luke Skywalker visit in *Star Wars*. Instead of having fully-animated creatures, all George could afford was rubber masks to stick over actors' heads.

So all the money *Star Wars* made was put into getting things better in the second movie, *The Empire Strikes Back*. In his first space movie, George got to create worlds no one had ever seen before. The next time around he got to improve on those other worlds. Instead of making twenty-five rubber masks that looked fake, he decided to make one really articulate creature: Yoda.

It was a creature that could move around freely and had a full range of facial expressions.

In the process of making *Star Wars*, George discovered something very important—he didn't like directing films. "I hate directing. It is like fighting a fifteen-round heavyweight bout with a new opponent every day," he said. "Making *Star Wars* nearly killed me." So he retired from directing, although he continues to be involved in filmmaking.

George wrote the stories for his other movies, and served as the producer. He would interview people to direct his movies, and once he had a new director, he would monitor the person's work. For *The Empire Strikes Back*, George hired Irvin Kershner, a director he admired for his ability to deal with human relationships.

George also kept a hand in his projects by serving as a film editor. "I started out in animation, and then I moved from animation to photography and then from photography to editing," he said. On most of his films, George does the final editing.

Soon after George began working on *Star Wars*, Francis Coppola began working on *Apocalypse Now*. When the picture was finally completed two years later, it was vastly different than the movie George once imagined. Francis did pay tribute to his friend in the Vietnam war movie. An intelligence officer who gives the hero his instructions early in the movie wears a name tag on his shirt that clearly reads "Col. G. Lucas."

George, however, used some of the ideas he originally had for *Apocalypse Now* in his own films. *More American Graffiti*, which George produced in 1968, used the low-budget, documentary style of filming that George had wanted to use in *Apocalypse*. And the final Ewok battle scene in *Return of the Jedi*, where the teddy bear-like creatures withstand all of the evil Empire's high technology, evolved from George's script of *Apocalypse Now*.

CREATING BOX OFFICE RECORDS

Back in 1977, right after *Star Wars* was released, George vacationed in Hawaii. He was joined by his friend, Steven Spielberg, whom George had known since 1967 when both men were in film school. Steven had gone to Long Beach State, but they had met through film festivals. Steven was in Hawaii waiting for *Close Encounters of the Third Kind,* his movie about visitors from outer space landing on earth, to be finished. The two men built a sand castle on the beach and talked about movies they would like to see made.

Spielberg told Lucas that he had always wanted to make a James Bond-adventure-type movie. George said he had a better idea, and told his friend about Indiana Jones, an archeologist and adventurer who saves the Lost Ark of the Covenant from Hitler. George's inspiration was from an old movie poster he had seen of a Zorro-like hero leaping from horseback to a traveling truck. He had had this idea before he made *Star Wars*.

George thought the movie should be based upon the awe-inspiring adventure serial matinees he used to see at the movies as a kid. In the serials, which were shown one chapter a week, a hero would get caught up in an adventure in an exotic land. Just before the chapter ended, the hero was usually in a dangerous situation

George Lucas with Irvin Kershner, whom he chose to direct *The Empire Strikes Back*, **and friend Steven Spielberg**

Harrison Ford played Indiana Jones in *Raiders of the Lost Ark*
and its sequel. George had first worked with Harrison in *American*
Graffiti, **then had called on him again for the role of Han Solo**
in the *Star Wars* **movies.**

from which it seemed he could not escape. The following
week he would make a miraculous escape and go on to
another adventure.

Steven loved the idea, and encouraged George to make
the movie. "No, I'm retired now," George said. "You
make it."

Back in Los Angeles, Steven, George, and a screenwriter
got together for five days, and with a tape recorder
running, George outlined his story in detail. Steven
took over the project, and directed *Raiders of the Lost*

A *Return of the Jedi* group shot: producer George Lucas, Han Solo (Harrison Ford), C-3PO (Anthony Daniels), Princess Leia (Carrie Fisher), Luke Skywalker (Mark Hamill), R2D2 (Kenny Baker), Chewbacca (Peter Mayhew), and director Richard Marquand

Ark. Lucas produced the movie, but his most valuable help came when the film needed to be edited. Steven made a rough cut of the movie, then turned it over to Lucas to do the final cut. The result far surpassed everyone's expectations. *Raiders of the Lost Ark* pulled in $115.5 million, putting it seventh on the list of top money-making moves of all time.

With *Raiders* in the works, George went back to his *Star Wars* saga, and hired a director to film the final chapter, *Return of the Jedi.* For this movie, George had the time and the money to make his imaginary world right. He created more than eighty creatures for the scene in Jabba the Hutt's shadowy palace. Jabba himself was the most complex, and largest, puppet ever created for a movie.

When it was completed, Steven Spielberg said he thought *Return of the Jedi* was the best *Star Wars* movie. It was also the most expensive, and had the most special effects.

Yet the fast pace of the movie does not allow the camera to dwell too long on the special effects. "Special effects are a way to tell a story, not a means unto themself," George has said. "Special effects by themself are boring." For this reason, George's films have a strong storyline and continuous action, and feature characters with real emotions.

RETIRED, BUT STILL ACTIVE

George Lucas is known throughout the movie industry as an honest man who still has the virtues his parents taught him: hard work is rewarded, and truth is the best policy. George gave cast and crew members of *American Graffiti* and *Star Wars* cash bonuses after he received the profits from the movies.

He has also been described as a man with a subtle sense of humor. He is reclusive when not working on movies, staying at home to watch television or listen to his large collection of early rock 'n' roll singles. For the most part, George shies away from the parties and lavish lifestyle many people associate with Hollywood directors. And George usually dresses the same way he did in film school: checked shirts, jeans or tan slacks, and tennis shoes.

Mark Hamill, who played Luke Skywalker in the *Star Wars* saga, recalls being invited over to Lucas's home one evening for dinner. When he arrived, he found out George's idea of going out to dinner was driving over to the local Taco Hut for a bite. "I should have known that George wouldn't go to a place with tablecloths and waiters."

Since the completion of the *Star Wars* saga, George Lucas has hardly been idle. The profits from *Star Wars* went into Lucasfilm, his film production company. The company has various divisions. Each division offers a service for other people who make movies. One such division is Industrial Light & Magic, a special effects research and production unit.

Industrial Light & Magic devised the special effects not only for George's three *Star Wars* films, but for Steven Spielberg's *E.T., Poltergeist, Raiders of the Lost Ark,* and for *Back to the Future* and *Young Sherlock Holmes,* which Spielberg produced. The special effects team also redesigned the rocket-ship ride in Disneyland, now named Star Tours. Much of ILM's trickery is developed to make inanimate figures, such as the creatures in *Jedi* and the stained-glass man in *Young Sherlock Holmes,* appear to move and act.

"Industrial Light & Magic is certainly the finest, in terms of special effects, in the world," said Jim Henson, the creator of the Muppets. In 1986, Henson and Lucas teamed up to make *Labyrinth,* a fantasy adventure

36

Jim Henson and George Lucas on the set of *Labyrinth*

that featured a number of Henson's creatures and
starred rock singer David Bowie.

George has also been working on setting up a facility
in which the film community can live and work, similar
to the situation he experienced while he was in film
school. The place is Skywalker Ranch, a complex of

almost 3,000 acres. It has an office complex with a library, screening rooms, recording studios, and sound stage areas in which filming can take place.

In 1985, George reunited with Francis Coppola to create a unique, three-dimensional musical presentation for Walt Disney World in Florida and Disneyland. The exhibit, titled *Captain EO*, features singer Michael Jackson in a space fantasy musical.

George Lucas and Michael Eisner, chairman and chief executive officer of the Walt Disney Co., cut the ribbon to open the new Star Tours ride at Disneyland — with a light saber, of course.

Although George has kept busy producing and editing movies, he has stayed true to his word about retiring from directing. He said, after *Empire Strikes Back* came out, that he would like to take some time to learn to play the guitar. He also said that he is interested in doing his "strange little experimental films" again.

Originally, *Star Wars* was conceived to run a total of nine chapters. Three more take place before the existing movies, and three after Luke and the rebels have overthrown the evil Empire. Now, however, it appears as if those films may never be made.

For over ten years, beginning in April of 1973 when George turned in his first story idea on *Star Wars* until the summer of 1983 when *Return of the Jedi* was released, George says there wasn't a day of his life that he didn't have to think about getting the movies finished. And he also had to worry about *Raiders of the Lost Ark* and *More American Graffiti* during the process. Because of that strain, he doesn't know if he will tackle another six chapters.

"Other people have said they think George is not going to do any more *Star Wars* films," Jim Henson said. During the time the two men worked together on *Labyrinth*, Henson said, the subject never came up.

Anthony Daniels, the British actor who played C-3PO in the three *Star Wars* movies, disagrees. "George is a very sensitive man, and I think he needs to know that the public wants to see another set of *Star Wars* movies," he said. "Of course, everyone I talk to does want to see them. But he needs to know that because there is a lot of work and a lot of money involved. And he needs to know that it is going to be worthwhile."

Whether or not the remaining chapters of *Star Wars* will be filmed, George Lucas shall always be remembered as one of Hollywood's most talented filmmakers. And future generations of movie audiences will be able to learn a bit about myths and legends from his works.